D1553294

The author of this book does not dispense medical advice or prescribe the use of any technique as a form of treatment of physical, emotional, or medical problems without the advice of a physician, either directly or indirectly. The intent of the author is only to offer information of a general nature to help you in your quest for emotional and spiritual well-being. In the event you use any of the information in the book for yourself, the author and the publisher assume no responsibility for your actions.

Table of Contents

Why I Wrote This Book

In 2015, I was bedridden. It took me years to get fully into my body and back to normal. I came out of this stronger energetically, emotionally, spiritually, and physically. I couldn't have done it without a regular practice of prayer and mantra recitation.

A month after I was sick, when I was in the early phase of recovery, a close aunt of mine was diagnosed with cancer. I had to take care of her while I was still shaky myself.

I was told by a spiritual leader that no doctor could save me, and that I had to practice mantra recitation every day. I would recite the mantra Waheguru (from darkness to light), twice a day for ten minutes with great focus. It worked then, and it has also worked many other times in my life.

When my health deteriorated, it was a regular connection with God and mantras that kept me going and healed me. I spent the days reading spiritual books that brought me hope, faith, trust, and miracles. I then read those to my suffering relatives as well who also found peace and hope.

Two years later, I was again tested by the downfall of another relative. I had to learn to protect my energy from others, so I joined the Psychic School, where I learned what was my energy and what was the energy of others. As a minister, I have realized that holding the space of prayers for others has always been my purpose and I had been fulfilling it since childhood. I just didn't know it was that deep of a calling while I was doing it.

It is thanks to these events during challenging times in my life and my connection with God that I am even able to write this book. If I had not had my own significant challenges, I wouldn't know resilience, perseverance, or how to deal with the difficulties we all currently face. If I hadn't had to overcome my fear of health crises and what could happen, I wouldn't be writing this book.

Whenever I was close to death or feeling down, in addition to praying, I danced. It was not in following others' moves that I healed, but in trusting the music to move me and to let my body find its own freedom and expression. It was simply being and allowing vs. doing. Dance like no one is watching. When we do what we desire and what our body wants, needs, or craves, we give into a power in between worlds beyond our ego and what keeps us separate to oneness. . . .and to what brings us life.

If you love doing something or have a practice you've been meaning to follow, I encourage you to pick that up now, as it could be a key first step in overcoming challenges that you are facing at this difficult time. Follow your heart, be gentle with yourself, and do everything you can to love yourself ten times more than you would normally.

Remember: No prayer is small. Ask for anything, even if it seems odd. Get in the habit of writing your own prayers. This is your divine time and you deserve to have it every day. This is a time to love yourself beyond your greatest imagination.

My hope is that through these prayers, you will be led to answers and miracles when you least expect them. I hope that you will find grace in this challenging time for yourself and those around you.

The Power of Prayer

What Is a Prayer and Why Pray?

A higher power connects us all. It is a part of us and around us. You can call it divine, supreme, Krishna, Jesus Christ, Guru Nanak, Allah, or simply a higher power. This higher power is unseen. In times of health crisis, and pandemics, we are forced to try measures we have not ever imagined. And, sometimes we don't know how.

I have personally experienced miracles several times in my life. Without these experiences, my life would not be where it is today. I have lived with a health crisis where I could not get out of bed. I have been handed tough situations in my life and without the strength from God, I would not have been able to stay sane.

I encourage you to try prayer. Miracles happen when we pray and believe there is a higher power holding us that wants to support us. Miracles happen when we don't give power to our difficult circumstances more than necessary. Miracles happen when we no longer stay in a position of powerlessness, but focus on hope, faith, trust, and surrender. We cannot see God the way we can feel money in our hands. It makes sense to be practical, but God is an unseen force that is here to support you. That is why you have to be willing to try, and to be open to what is possible.

Be willing to notice and sit after your prayers with closed eyes and no judgment. Allow the higher power of your choice to heal you. Ask for whatever you need. There is no right or wrong. I speak to God like a best friend and share all that I feel before or after reading the prayers. Afterwards, I close my eyes and let God heal me. God can be your best friend during your darkest times. When you sit with God, you might cry. Allow yourself to be cleansed. No prayer is too small or too big. Create a list of what works for you.

Everyone can write a prayer. You can customize your prayers to work for you and your situations. It is a matter of habit and surrender. Mostly, it is having faith and trusting the process of your prayers.

Building A Relationship With God

Building a relationship with God is a practice like anything else. It requires that we set aside time to pray, write out our prayers, read them, listen to our guidance, and allow healing to take place. It requires you to release control, surrender to the flow of prayers as you pray, and be open to what happens as a result of praying. It requires you allow a beautiful power of love to heal you. You must trust that your prayers are heard and be open to how they unfold in your healing. Make the prayers a daily process and don't give up. Let your prayers change and evolve. Sit with God as much as you can. Talk to God like your best friend or as you write in your favorite journal. Be gentle with yourself.

Creating A Sacred Time And Space For God

It helps to have a sacred altar or an area in your home dedicated only to God. You can light a candle, burn incense, or have your favorite holy book-anything authentic that resonates with your heart. You can also go to the prayer room in a hospital. Find a corner that feels safe for you or even outside in nature. I believe God is especially present in our darkest times, but we need to believe, trust, and have faith. There are unexpected blessings during these darkest times. Be willing to notice what happens.

Commitment and Dedication

If we don't dedicate time to physical exercise, it won't happen. Prayers, too, need time, space, and dedication. We must not give up when our prayers are not answered immediately. We must have faith and trust that while some prayers may be answered, others might not, and some may be answered later. When I pray consistently, I have breakthroughs and sometimes shifts in my perception. My prayers evolve over time as my inner world grows. We must be open to hearing the answers in ways we least expect. I have had prayers answered months after praying. The answers have come in unexpected ways and have been some of my greatest blessings. In times of continuous loss in my life, I have asked God to show me the silver lining in each loss. When we can see that, our world begins to shift.

Answered Prayers

To boost our faith and remember our trust in the higher power, we must keep a journal to remind ourselves of the power of having faith and surrendering to this higher power. It is easy to forget this when things are hard. Our ego takes over, wants us to separate from our higher power and oneness with all that is, and gives more power to our pain, sadness, grief, anger, and fears. We are humans after all. If you have this experience, simply forgive yourself and start over when you can. I encourage you to start praying when you are ready and keep it up.

Pay It Forward

If you find leaning on prayers makes a difference in your life, please pay it forward by sharing your wisdom, and this book, with at least one person. You never know why someone might need prayers. It could be life changing.

An Important Note

Please know that I am not a doctor and you should take all precautions necessary to maintain your health. The prayers are here for you to have faith during a time of great uncertainty in this world. I hope you find peace, ease, hope, and grace during this time.

Self-Care

Dear God,

Teach me how to love myself and to take very good care of my body, energy, and immune system. Send me the support and resources that I need to remain safe.

Dear God,

Please teach me how to be with myself and to love myself. Please help me to not affect others through all the mixed emotions I am going through. Help me to find healthy ways to cope, to feel, and to release my emotions by finding outlets like journaling, dancing, singing, or even beating up a pillow. Teach me how to do this and help me create a healthy routine of loving all these aspects of myself.

Dear God,

Please show me creative ways to keep myself happy and my energy high, not low. Release me from the addiction of spending time on things that bring me down. Help me to be open to what brings me happiness, peace, ease, and contentment.

Dear God,

I keep cleaning and sanitizing. I keep giving up what I need for my family's sake. Please help me to put myself first and to look at what I am avoiding within myself. I know that when I feel whole and self-connected, I am able to give back even more.

Dear God,

I have lost my path and am not able to continue what I was working on before all this happened. I am distracted easily while taking care of my family's needs. Among all this, please show me how to put myself first and to make time to do what is most important for me.

Reminder of Inner Strength

Dear God,

Remind me of all the times I have persevered through difficult times and of my innate strength. Help me to know and believe that I have always come out stronger and that I will do so this time, too.

Dear God,

Please help me find comfort, create a new routine and feel ease and joy in it.

Dear God,

For my well-being, please help me to find humor and to laugh daily.

Dear God,

I have been in denial of what is going on. Please help me to accept and surrender to what is going on and, and trust that this situation will help me and everyone in the long run. Help me to face it, and not to run away. Help me to take each moment of each day in baby steps. Please guide me.

Dear God,

Please help me to love and accept all of myself and start all over again. Help me to forgive myself for any mistakes I made during the day. This is a tough time. Please teach me how to be gentle and kind with myself.

Dear God,

Please help me to feel joy and pleasure during this time. Help my whole family move from fear to joy. Help us to believe that we deserve to have fun, to play, and to enjoy our lives–no matter what the circumstances. Help us to know we are safe and protected.

Dear God,

Please help me to practice unconditional love for myself and others.

Dear God,

Please help me to have patience and resilience through this time. Remind me of my strength and ability carry on no matter what.

Hydration and Immune Strength

Dear God,

Please help me to stay hydrated and build the strength to be immune to this disease.

Dear God,

No matter what happens, help me to stay calm, to be at ease, to pray, and to prepare for everything.
Help me to have faith and trust that all will be okay.
Help me to know I am blessed, and that I will get through this.

Dear God,

Please help those searching for a cure to find the cure easily and rapidly. Help us to all have a cure sooner rather than later. We thank you.

Loss and Grief

Dear God,

I have lost people in my family and/or friends. Please help me feel the grief while keeping me safe and protected. Help me not to give up or be reckless with my own health. Boost my faith and trust in life, and help me to know that I will get through this experience. Help me to trust that I will be stronger on the other side. Walk with me each step of the way. Help me to know I am held, safe, and supported during this time.

Dear God,

Please bless everyone in fear and grief. Help them overcome this with bravery and strength. Help them find the support they need.

Dear God,

The world is in loss and I am in loss. Please help me to heal and help the world to heal. Help us to rise together and stronger. Help us all overcome this difficult time and come out stronger on the other side.

Dear God,

Many businesses have lost money, clients, or workers, and have been forced to shut down. Please help them find other ways to have money. Help them to know they are blessed with abundance. Help them to find creative ways to channel their loss and grief, and to find the support they need during this time.

Dear God,

I have lost all my normal activities, and I have no job or business. Please help me to heal and feel the grief. Give me the strength to start all over again, and to be creative. Give me money and strength to sustain myself during this time. Help me to know that this, too, will pass. Keep my spirits high and help me to start all over again. Please be with me during this time and show me the silver lining in all of this.

Dear God,

Many people have lost or are afraid of losing their jobs. Help them to channel their energy in healthy and positive ways and shower them with abundance and creative means to get through this time. Show them their strength, especially now, and their ability to carry on.

Loss of Control and Uncertainty

Dear God,

I know this situation is asking me to change and be different. Help me to get quiet enough to listen to you and let go of what no longer works for me.

Dear God,

Please help me build a new relationship with uncertainty and change. Help me to release all fear of what will or will not happen. Help me to be stronger and to have the courage and strength to accept all that comes my way.

Dear God,

In this situation, I feel powerless to help myself and those who need me. Help me to have faith and trust that this, too, shall pass, and all will be okay in due time. Help others know the same.

Breathe Through Loss of Control

Dear God,

Please help me to breathe through my fear of the unknown, and my anxiety, loss of control, fear, and unrest. Help me to sit with all this and teach me how to be with all these emotions in a loving way.

Overcoming Fears

Dear God,

At any given time, it is easy to succumb to the fear and anxiety caused by lack of resources and what will happen. Please fill me with choosing joy over sadness, happiness over fear, hope over hopelessness, and love and miracles over anything that brings me down.

Dear God,

Please help me to remove all paranoia regarding this virus. Help me feel calm and ease. Release me from all agitation.

Dear God,

Please lift me from negativity and fear. Transform my fear into love, peace, ease, calm, and happiness. Help me to feel safe and secure. Help me to know that I am and have always been enough. Help me to know that I am protected and all will be well.

Dear God,

I am afraid. I am scared. Why am I going through all this? Help me instill my trust and faith in this Universe. Help me to know that this world is a good place and that we are just having a challenging time. Help me to stay positive and to know that I will get through this. Boost my faith, my trust in you, and my hope, now more than ever.

Release Victimhood

Dear God,

Help me to know that I am not a victim of this pandemic. Release me from any fear and help me to feel whole and complete as I take all precautions.

Dear God,

Please help heal all the fear that I carry and transform it into knowing and trusting that I am safe. Help me to know that I will get through this and will be stronger than ever before.

Issues with Home and Work

Dear God,

Please help me to connect with others and to feel engaged and involved through communication channels while practicing social distancing.

Finding Space at Home For Myself

Dear God,

Please help me to find space for myself at home. I miss my space and the freedom to do what I want, whenever I want, and to go wherever I want. Help me to get through this time feeling free and at ease.

Dear God,

I am bored at home. Help me to shift this into fun and find interesting things to do while staying home, safe, and protected. Help me overcome boredom. I need you.

Tired Sick And Frustrated

Dear God,

I am frustrated, and sick and tired of staying at home. Please give me extra strength and courage to get through this. I need you.

Dear God,

I don't know where to start. Please guide me to build healthy habits from home, get along with others, and enjoy the process.

Dear God,

Teach me how to cooperate with the rules and regulations, both external and in my home, so that I can stay safe physically, as well as emotionally and mentally healthy. Help me to know that this, too, shall pass.

Dear God,

I really don't want to be around. Things have been so tough. I don't know how to cope with this. Please show me and teach me that I matter, and that I am not a victim of this world or those around me. Help me not to give up. Intervene and stop me. Shine your light on me to get me out of this darkness.

Dear God,

I have lost the space in which I normally practice or teach. I have lost connection with others and I need help with my students. I need help finding purpose, meaning, and satisfaction. Help me to achieve all this while at home while staying safe. Help me to use this time to be even more creative and resourceful and be there for all those who need me. Help me uncover my hidden passions and talents and put them to great use.

Dear God,

I really miss my normal activities and I want to go out. Help me to have the discipline, inner strength, and trust to know all will be well soon and not to give up. Help me to stay safe now.

Dear God,

Thank you for helping me not to give into temptations. Thank you for giving me the ability to save lives by not getting infected myself, by staying home, and being protected. Help me to know there are opportunities, and I can be productive, healthy, and happy from home. I look forward to joining the community soon.

Dear God,

I am suffering to need to find time and space for myself. Help me to find this time for myself among all that is going on right now. Let me be true to myself, so that I may do things that make me feel purposeful, satisfied, and happy. Help me to be connected to my deepest self. Show me the way. Guide me to do this over the next few months.

Dear God,

I have suddenly gone from being busy to doing nothing. Help me to feel useful, needed, meaningful, and satisfied while I am going through this transition of being at home. Help me to be open to new routines while creating new healthy habits.

Dear God,

I am feeling lonely. Please help me to know that I am not alone. Give me the courage to reach out and connect with others and to feel like I am never separate from them.

Dear God,

Please help me to adjust, cope, manage my relationships and work in such a confined space. Help us all to create new routines that support our productivity, health, need for space, rest, food, sleep, inner peace, and happiness.

Dear God,

Please make my home a conflict-free zone. Help everyone to stay calm, healthy, and happy, and to respect each other's spaces. Help us to bring out the best in each other and not the worst.

After Reading the News

Dear God,

Please help me not to give into any fears and to stay mentally strong and positive.

Fear of Isolation

Dear God,

I am afraid of isolation and I hate it. Please help me to overcome this and to know that I am never truly alone and that we are all one, together, and always connected.

Fear of Suffocation

Dear God,

I feel suffocated at home and it is quite frustrating. Help me to feel free within and to breathe through all of this.

Dear God,

I don't know how I will spend all this time alone. Please help me to feel more connected with others via phone, email, and online media. Help me to know I am never alone.

Health:
Staying Healthy

Dear God,

Please help me to be prepared with all the resources and medications I need, in case I do get infected.

Preparation for Food and Medicines

Dear God,

Please help me to have enough food, water, medicines and resources I might need to stay safe and prepare for what might be coming my way.

Dear God,

I already live with existing health issues. I am even more scared of what might come . Please always keep me strong and healthy. Please make sure I have all the medications and resources that I might need. Help me to feel extra safe and to know that this, too, shall pass.

Dear God,

I have no choice, I must go to the doctor. Keep me safe and protected from all those affected by the virus and other diseases. Keep me safe under your care as I go through the next steps.

Dear God,

I need my daily exercise to keep my heart and body healthy. Show me how to move my body in new ways that brings me joy and good health throughout this difficult time.

Dear God,

Since I have been at home, I have been getting fat and eating or drinking in an unhealthy way. Help me to overcome the root cause of these issues and finally set myself free. Help me to trust the process, and make healthy choices every day, and to forgive myself for any unhealthy choices I have made at any step along the way.

Dear God,

I am already going through depression and staying at home makes me feel even worse. Help me to find a new routine at home that is safe and heals me in many ways. Help me to find joy and comfort.

Health:
When Sick

Dear God,

Please help keep my lungs and respiratory system strong and working efficiently, and prevent me from getting sicker. Help me to breathe normally. Show me your miracles and help everyone around me to believe and trust that I will be okay.

When I Am Sick

Dear God,

Please help me to heal and recover soon. Help me to get healthy quickly. Help me to know I am safe and protected. Bless me.

Dear God,

I have tested positive. I need you by my side. Please help me to overcome this, stay strong, heal as soon as possible, not be scared, and not give it more power than it deserves. Help me to have all the resources and the support that I need. Show me your miracles. I am open to receiving them.

Dear God,

I don't know how I am going to make it out of this experience of getting the virus. Guide me. Support me every step of the way so that I don't feel alone, isolated, or helpless. Help me to feel strong emotionally, mentally, physically, psychically, and energetically. Help me to trust the process and have insurmountable faith. Help me to feel supported and taken care of no matter what happens. Help me to accept what is happening and to feel all my emotions. Help me to heal and know that my body and soul are one and that I am never, ever separated from anyone. Teach me how to pray every day and each step of the way.

Keeping Family Safe

Dear God,

Please help my family stay safe and secure and help them not to get ill from contact with me.

Dear God,

Please don't let the virus from spread from me to others.

Dear God,

Release me from the guilt that I carry that I may have done things that might have spread the virus. Keep me emotionally, physically, and mentally strong. Help me always to keep my faith and trust.

Health:

Dying

Dear God,

I am dying, and I don't know what to do. Show me the way that where I am going is also a beautiful place. Help me not to be attached to any form and to know that I am going to a place of love and oneness. Help me to be released from the fear of death. Help me to release the fear of losing all those whom I leave behind, including my family, friends, connections, and the experiences of being in a body.

Fear of Dying

Dear God,

I am afraid of dying. I don't want to die. If I must die, let me know and trust that on the other side there are beautiful things and that I will never be truly separate from others. If I am to survive, show me great courage and strength to come out of this stronger and healthier than ever before.

Families

Dear God,

Please bless, heal, and be with all the families and souls that are affected by the virus. Help them to know that they are supported and taken care of. Give them faith. Give them hope. Help them to know that this, too, shall pass.

Prayer for the Safety and Harmony of the Family

Dear God,

Please help me and my family stay safe, secure, and in harmony during this difficult time.

Prayer for Kids

Dear God,

Please help keep my children safe, secure, and healthy. I am really worried about them. Help me to remove my worries and fears and to trust that all will be okay.

Prayer for Elders

Dear God,

I have aging parents, and I am scared and worried about them. Help them to stay safe, secure and protected. Help them to have good hygiene, enough food, and great health. Help them to feel supported and safe.

Dear God,

I am really worried this virus is going to take me away. They say it is us who are at most risk. Please be by my side and help me overcome all my fears, worries, and anxieties. Keep me safe and healthy. Help me to know and trust that I already have all the support and resources I need.

Dear God,

My partner and/or my children do not believe in God. They are negative and in fear. Please help them to stay calm and peaceful and help boost their faith. Don't let their energy affect mine. Help them to stay happy and healthy during this time.

Dear God,

I am really worried about my family. They don't live with me. I am afraid they are going to die, and I am not even with them. Help them to be safe and secure. Help them to have all the resources and support they need at this crucial time. Remove my anxiety and fears about losing them. Please God, I pray to you. Thank you.

Dear God,

I have teenagers at home who are in denial and are rebelling. I need your help to step in and support them. Help them hear your messages in ways that work for them. Help them to stay safe and protected in all ways.

Getting Around

Staying Safe When Going to The Grocery Store or Receiving Home Deliveries

Dear God,

Please keep me safe when I go into grocery stores and when I receive food that has been delivered to my home. Release and protect me from anything that brings the virus close to me.

Dear God,

I must go out and I have no choice. Please guide my steps to go where it is safe and not where it is unsafe. Help me to have gloves, masks, and the wisdom to make healthy choices for myself and for everyone else involved.

Dear God,

Please make the process of deliveries for stores, for those doing the deliveries, and for those of us receiving them to be safe and secure.

Relationships

Difficulty with My Partner

Dear God,

It has been very difficult to be with my partner at this time. It is impossible to be around him or her. I don't have anywhere else to go, as the disease is everywhere. Step in to my home and heal us, so we can be kind and respectful towards each other. Remove the fear and the darkness that surrounds us, so we can cooperate and let go of the negativity within and around us.

Dear God,

I cannot stand my partner or housemate. Please remove all obstacles that are making us fight, stay in our egos, and remain separate from each other. Help us to have peace and harmony. Thank you for healing us separately and together. Help us to know that we are not alone, and all this will be over soon.

Dear God,

I am overwhelmed by all the issues with my partner, because we are suddenly forced to be together for so long. Please help us both to stay calm and face our issues while we learn to live together. Help us to find harmony and inner strength not to hurt each other, but instead to create more joy, peace, and ease in being together. Help us to take turns in cooking, cleaning, help each other out, and have our own time to breathe.

Abuse

Dear God,

I am being abused at home and I don't know what to do. With my partner home all the time, I am scared and I don't have any time to myself. Please always step into my home and be with my family. Be my guardian and protector, and work your miracles.

Dear God,

My workday is tough, and I have nowhere to vent anymore, since I am at home all the time. Please help me not to take my tough day and emotions out on my family. Help me to find healthy outlets to release and vent.

Challenging Times

Dear God,

In this challenging time, be by my side and send me miracles. Send me love. Send me kindness. Help me to know that I am supported. Show me how not to give up and stay strong. Show me how to come out of this experience stronger and braver than ever before. Show me the light at the end of the tunnel. Keep me close.

Crisis

Dear God,

Please help me get through this crisis. Help me to know what I am learning and how best to show up and feel supported and safe throughout.

Dear God,

Please help everyone who is struggling and suffering because of the virus find ease, comfort, rest, hope, faith, and a connection with others.

Care for Those Who are Sick

Dear God,

Please help all those who are sick to have the support, resources, and care that they need. Lift their spirits high and help them to know all will be okay.

Dear God,

This is a very shocking and difficult time for me and everyone. Please show us the silver lining in all of this.

Positive Upliftment and Cure

Dear God,

Help me to make an impact on others as I am going through the Coronavirus challenge. Help me to shine my light and help others. Help me to know that my impact, no matter how small it is, matters.

Dear God,

Bless me to pray for all. Help me to serve while keeping myself safe and healthy. Please use me as a beacon of light to spread light and goodness.

Gratitude for Being Healthy

Dear God,

Thank you for keeping me healthy during this time. I am ever so grateful for your blessings and all that I do have.

Dear God,

I know you are the magic worker full of miracles, love, and blessings. Please help the world find a cure now and thank you for showering us with your unconditional blessings always.

To Be the Light

Dear God,

Please help me to be the light. Help me to spread happiness, positivity, dance, fun, humor, calm, strength, courage, and bravery, instead of more worry, fear, and anxiety.

Dear God,

Please help me spread movement from home by inspiring and uplifting others through dance, exercise, yoga, and more.

Spreading Laughter

Dear God,

Please help me to spread laughter, fun, and play while being of service.

Dear God,

Please help me to spread inspiration and motivation from home.

Focus on Joy

Dear God,

Please help me to focus on what brings me great joy. Release the energy of others and of the media away from me. Keep me, my housemates, and my family safe and protected while we focus on inner calm, joy, and peace.

Dear God,

Please help me to know and realize all that I currently have in my life, as opposed to what I don't have. Help me to feel gratitude, even among this chaos, and to count my blessings.

Dear God,

Please help me to surrender to things that bring me great healing like music, dance, laughter, and prayers.

Starting and Ending the Day

Prayer Upon Waking

Dear God,

Thank you for blessing me with this day. Bless this day to bring me ease, comfort, peace, and joy. Help me to stay happy, healthy, positive, and calm.

Dear God,

Please be with me during my sleep. Keep me safe and protected and let no harm or fear come my way. Keep my vibration high and happy. Help me to get deep rest and wake up into another beautiful sunshiny day.

Hospital, Healthcare Providers, and Essential Workers

Hospitals and Resources

Dear God,

Please help all the hospitals have enough ventilators, testing kits, and all resources they need to do what is the highest good for all those affected.

Dear God,

Please help all hospital workers to have enough energy, nutrition, health, rest, focus, faith, trust, and optimism. Keep them safe, protected, strong, supported, and grounded. Bless them for working so hard during this time.

Dear God,

There is a shortage of masks, testing kits, ventilators, gloves, disinfectants and more. Please take extra care of the doctors, nurses, and hospital staff that are doing the best they can to take care of their patients. Help everyone who needs protection to have what they need. Keep them extra safe and blessed.

Dear God,

Bless all the souls that are working and supporting all of us while we are at home. Help them to stay safe and healthy. Bless them for being of service to all of us. Keep them healthy and safe wherever they are.

Public Officials and Leaders

For City, Country, and International Officials

Dear God,

Please help all city, country, and world officials to make choices effectively and efficiently and to take the responsibility for doing what is right. Help them guide them to make decisions that will bring the highest good for all.

Countries

Dear God,

Please help all countries cooperate and support each other during this time when we all need each other.

Dear God,

Please support all leaders and guide them to be knowledgeable, and trustworthy, and to write and speak the words that have the highest and most positive impact on everyone. Help them to rise to be their best.

Faith and Trust in The Universe

Dear God,

I have lost faith and trust in this Universe. These are difficult times and everyone around me is struggling. Is it safe to be here? Do I want to be here? How can you let this happen? Please help me to have the strength to overcome the current circumstances and know that I will come out stronger from this experience. Please help me to find the silver lining in this experience. Boost my faith and trust in this Universe to be much higher than any fear I see around and within me. Help me to know that this world is a good place having a hard time.

Finding Hope

Dear God,

It is easy to lose hope with the current circumstances. Please help me to know that this is a good world having a difficult time.

I Don't Believe In God

Dear God,

I have never really believed in you. Religion was forced on me. I ended up rebelling. I don't want to be controlled. I don't want to be punished. Is there a loving God? Can God be a part of me? Teach me a new relationship with you. I give up. Get me out of this rebellion and help me to build a safe and loving relationship with you that is not like what I was taught when I was young.

Dear God,

I need your help to guide me on how to hear my own answers and how to hear you. Please guide me on how to do this.

The New World

After the Crisis

Dear God,

Please help me to be prepared for what is coming after the virus is done and the crisis is over. Help me to get ready mentally, emotionally, physically, and financially for the new world.

About The Author

Manpreet Komal is a spiritual leader. She is a minister and a graduate of Psychic Horizons and has completed more than three hundred readings and healings in the last three years. Manpreet has mentored for the Ford Institute as a Certified Shadow Coach, and has been published in three international best-selling books. She has written a Self Love Column for South Asian Woman magazine and has a following of 140,000 people on social media. Manpreet runs Rang De Bollywood Dance Company, where she empowers and motivates others to overcome challenges with their mental and physical health through dance. She studies dance, writing, and spirituality, as well as making her own contributions to these fields.

www.manpreetkomal.org
www.rangdebollywood.com

Follow her writing on Facebook at:
www.facebook.com/universesendshelp

Instagram at:
instagram.com/manpreetbreakthroughcoach

Made in the USA
Middletown, DE
05 September 2020

17209337R00085